THE HOCKEY PLAYER'S COOKBOOK

Brandon Aldan

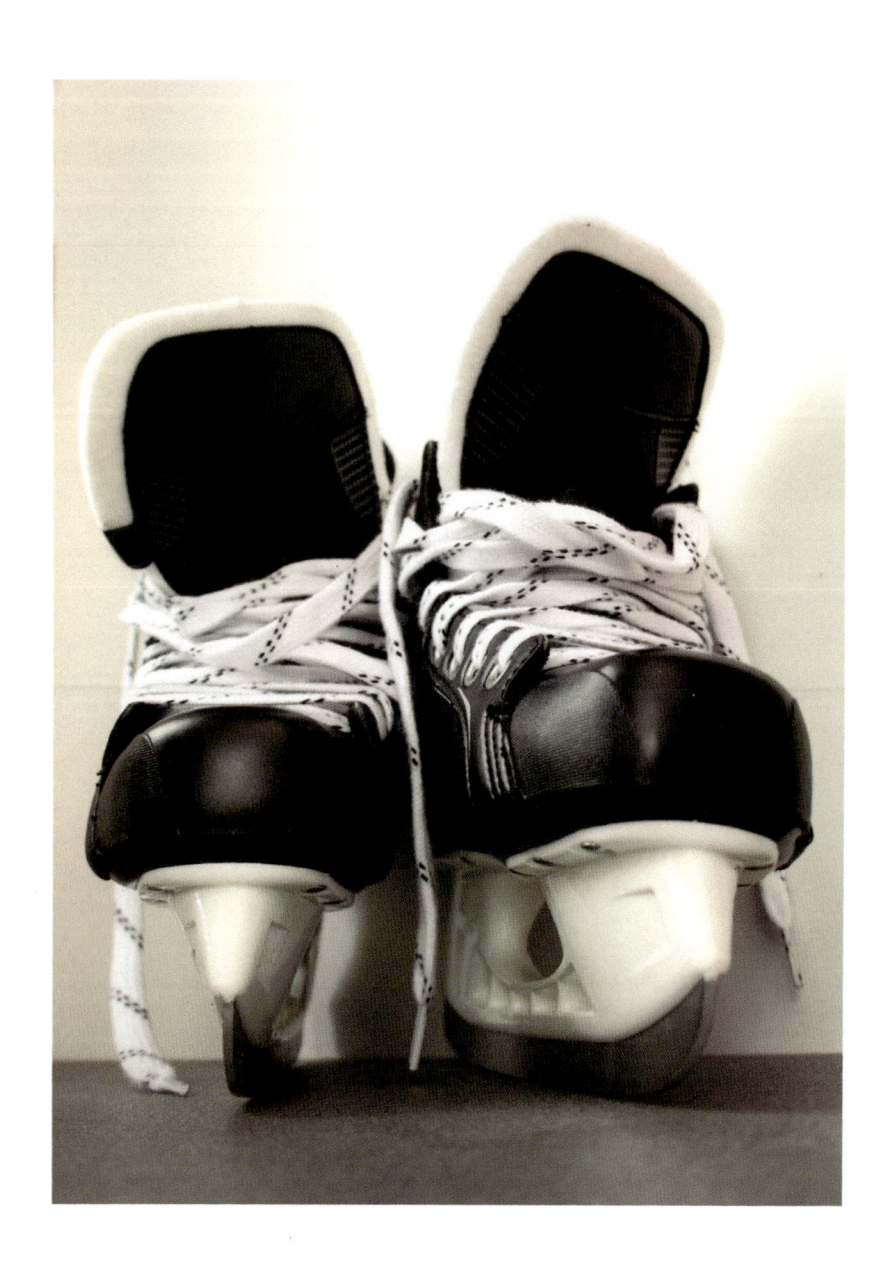

Copyright © 2012 Brandon Aldan
All rights reserved.
ISBN-13: 978-1481002783

CONTENTS

Introduction	1
Basic Nutrition	2
Sample Meal Plans	6
Basic Cooking	7
Grocery Shopping	8
Breakfast	10
Lunch	21
Pre-Workout	33
Post-Workout	39
Pre-Game	44
Dinner	50
Healthy Snacks	60
Cheat Meals	68
Eating on the Road	73

INTRODUCTION

I've been training athletes for over 18 years and one of the most difficult influencers of performance for me to correct is diet. The importance of diet cannot be overstated. A hockey player's body is like a high performance machine. The type and amount of fuel you put in are extremely important to how you play. Good nutrition can enhance focus, raise energy, expedite recovery and improve overall performance.

Hockey players face many obstacles when trying to get adequate nutrition. Youth players lack any education of what healthy foods are and their diets are mainly left to the discretion of their parents or what is available at the rink. Junior players have trouble fitting healthy eating into their rough schedule of practice, sleeping and playing XBox. College athletes have to juggle classes, practice, games, travel, etc. while mixing in meals which are quick and cheap. Adult hockey players have to consider late ice times, family schedule, and work.

The intention of this cookbook is to provide hockey players and parents with healthy recipes that are relatively inexpensive and somewhat easy to make. I've also included some more complicated meals that require little more cooking ability than knowing how to read instructions.

BASIC NUTRITION

A good diet is essential to fuel maximum performance. Diet affects energy levels throughout the day as well as training intensity. Proper nutrition is also very important for recovery and repair of tissues damaged during training.

Carbohydrates: This is the primary source of fuel for hockey. Complex carbohydrates from whole grains are the preferred source. Refined sugars should be avoided. Fruits and vegetables should be eaten daily. To calculate daily carbohydrate needs multiply weight x 2 to 2.5 = grams carbohydrate.

Good sources: Whole wheat bread, oatmeal, barley, whole grain pasta, brown rice, quinoa, fruits, sweet potatoes

Fats: Fats are necessary for various functions in the body including, energy production and vitamin absorption. Most fats should be in the form of monounsaturated or polyunsaturated fat. These fats can have a positive effect on health. Saturated fats with the exception of coconut oil should be kept low. To calculate daily fat needs multiply weight x 0.5 to 0.7 = grams fat per day.

Good sources: olive oil, avocados (great in guacamole), canola oil, coconut oil or coconut milk, flax seeds and flax oil, almonds, walnuts, pumpkin seeds

Protein: Protein is used to build and repair tissues particularly, muscle tissue. Hockey players require more protein than the average person but, excess protein goes unused by the body and is excreted. To calculate protein needs multiply weight x 0.8 to 1.1 = grams protein per day.

Good sources: lowfat milk, chicken, turkey, lean beef, bison, whey powder, eggs, tuna, wild salmon, Greek yogurt

Vitamins and minerals: Vitamins and minerals are necessary for many bodily functions such as, energy production and tissue health. Most vitamins and minerals can be obtained through a balanced diet with good variety of nutrient-dense foods like fruits and vegetables but, a daily multi-vitamin is recommended to ensure all needs are met.

Water: Considering that our bodies are 60-70% water, this is the most important nutrient. Even slight dehydration can lead to muscle cramps, decreased concentration and impaired neuromuscular performance. Drink 8-10 eight ounce glasses of fluid, preferably water, each day.

GENERAL NUTRITION TIPS

Choose foods with high nutrient density. Nutrient density means the food provides many vitamins, minerals, and antioxidants per calorie. Avoid empty calorie foods like soda, candy, etc. These foods have very low nutrient density.

Choose whole foods over processed, refined foods. Nutrients such as, vitamins and minerals are best absorbed from the original food source.

Eat a large variety of vegetables and eat vegetables at every meal. Vegetables are great snacks between meals.

It can be difficult to eat healthy at school and work so pack your own lunches or snacks. A few extra minutes a day preparing a lunch can make a major impact on your overall diet which will enhance performance.

Choose hormone-free, free-range, grass-fed meats. These meats are much healthier and can provide more omega 3 fatty acids.

Choose organic when possible especially for fruits and vegetables. Some fruits and vegetables have more resilient skins and most pesticides can be removed by washing. Consult a chart online to see which ones are most important to buy organically.

A handful of nuts make a great snack. Nuts provide healthy fats and provide nutrient-dense calories.

Learn to read labels. Look up any substances you've never heard of. Avoid artificial colors, flavors and sweeteners. These substances are toxic and may be responsible for many health problems. Also avoid hydrogenated oils and high fructose corn syrup.

Fix your diet before adding supplements. Certain supplements such as, creatine and beta alanine have shown to enhance performance but, will not make up for poor nutrition. Correcting nutrient deficiencies will have a much greater impact on performance than any supplement.

Most athletes don't get enough fiber, vitamin D, and omega 3 fatty acids. Add fiber to many meals by using The Fiber 35 Diet Sprinkle Fiber. You can also easily mix this in to shakes. I would recommend taking 5000 IU's of vitamin D per day in the form of a softgel. You can get additional omega 3 fatty acids by adding flax and chia seeds to many meals or by taking it in softgels.

Don't wait until you're thirsty to drink. By this point, you are already slightly dehydrated. Drink 8-10 8 ounce glasses of fluids consisting mostly of water throughout the day.

Sweating while playing and training requires replacement of electrolytes in addition to fluid. BioSteel High Performance Sports Drink and NOOMA are my personal choices during during training. For games, I add a couple tablespoons of cane sugar. Coconut water is also a great natural electrolyte replacement.

Juice is better than soda but, still contains a lot of sugar. Dilute 100% fruit juice with equal parts filtered water.

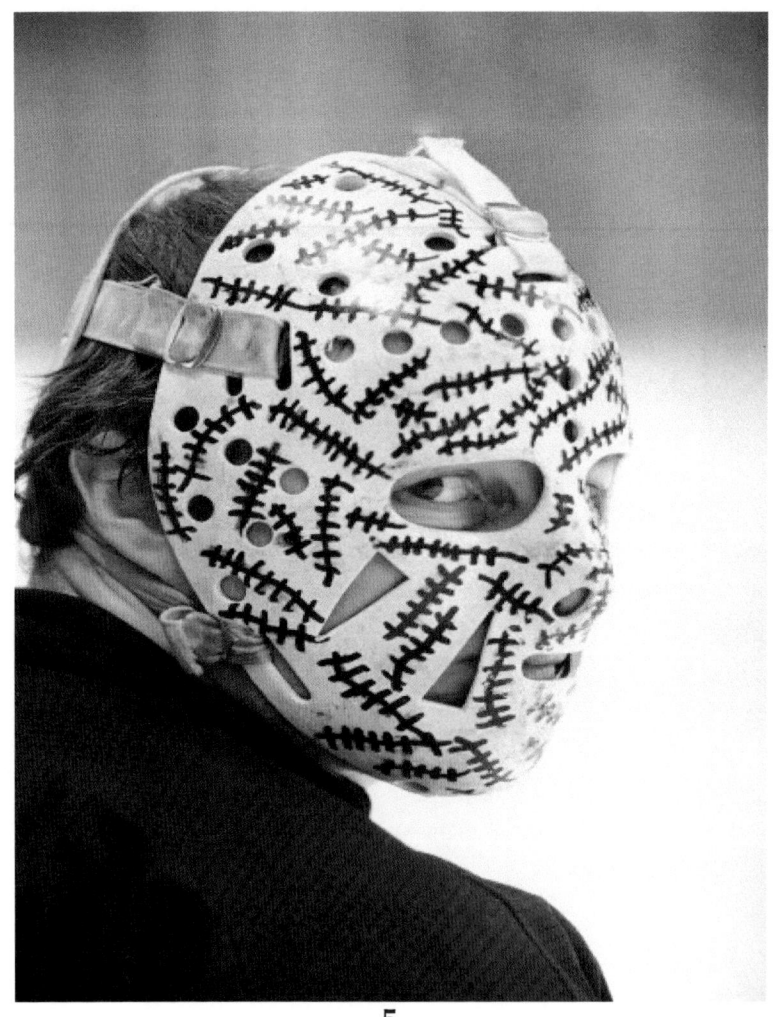

SAMPLE MEAL PLAN 1

Great for a player trying to gain weight

Breakfast- Protein Oatmeal

Lunch- Elvis Sandwich

Pre-workout- Coconut whey shake

During workout- BioSteel High Performance Drink

Post-workout- Pumpkin Pie Smoothie

Dinner- Sausage Meatloaf

Nighttime snack- Late Night Anabolic Snack

SAMPLE MEAL PLAN 2

Breakfast- Yogurt and Cottage Cheese

Lunch- Buttery Fava Beans

Pre-workout- Boiled Sweet Potato

During workout- BioSteel High Performance Drink

Post-workout- BioSteel Advanced Recovery

Dinner- Lemon Chicken and Brown Rice

Nighttime snack- Brandon's Tasty Treats

BASIC COOKING

Cooking can seem daunting to those who haven't tried before but, especially for the recipes in this book, it is mostly following directions. Burning food is a common rookie mistake. Check food regularly to avoid burning. Don't just leave your food to cook on its own. Another common mistake is incorrect measurements. Especially, make sure you don't get tablespoons (Tbsp) and teaspoons (tsp) confused.
Before you start, set out everything you will need as far as ingredients and cooking tools. Clean up and put things away as you are done with them so you don't have a huge mess to clean up at the end.
Wash hands very thoroughly after touching raw meat and poultry to avoid spreading harmful bacteria. Also, clean any surface or cooking tool they come in contact with.
The recipes in this book are just guidelines. Don't be afraid to experiment and change recipes.

Tools you will need;
Frying pan
Baking dish
Cooking sheet
Metal pot
Metal whisk
Wooden spoon
Measuring cups
Measuring spoons
Blender
Toaster
Slow cooker (optional)

GROCERY SHOPPING

I recommend Trader Joe's and Whole Foods for most groceries. Trader Joe's has great prices on natural and organic Foods but, has a fairly limited selection so you might not find everything you need. Whole Foods has a reputation for being expensive but, this is mostly due to carrying many exotic specialty foods. They also have their Whole Foods 365 brand for most products which is very reasonably priced for organic and natural foods.

Make a list and stick to it. I go to Trader Joe's first then head over to Whole Foods for the rest of the items on my list. At either store, shop the perimeter first where you will find all the most important staples such as, meats, eggs, milk, seafood, fruits and vegetables. Stick to your list and only go to the aisles you need to avoid buying unnecessary items. It helps to arrange your list by aisle.

Also, don't go grocery shopping when you're hungry. Otherwise, you will come out of there spending way more than you meant to.

Brandon's Shopping List

Fage Total 2% Greek yogurt
Earth Balance buttery spread
Free range omega 3 eggs
Free range chicken breasts
Organic quick oats
TJ's organic tricolor quinoa
Fiber 365 Diet sprinkle fiber
BioSteel High Performance Drink
Westbrae Natural fava beans
Allegro Coffee drinking chocolate
Apple juice sweetened cranberries
Bob's Red Mill chia seeds
Semi-sweet chocolate chips

Earth Balance coconut spread
Grass fed free range beef
365 organic whole milk
Shredded unsweetened coconut
TJ's wasabi roasted seaweed snack
Organic dark cocoa powder
BioSteel whey isolate
BioSteel Advanced Recovery
Eternal Water alkaline bottled water
Organic raisins
Truvia sweetener
Bob's Red Mill flax seeds
Agave nectar

Yellow onions	Gala apples
Coconut oil	Extra virgin olive oil
Organic strawberries	Organic blueberries
Almond Butter	Grass fed butter
Wild caught canned tuna	Free range grass fed top sirloin
Free range grass fed ground beef	Bananas
Wild caught cod	Wild caught salmon
Frozen broccoli	Frozen peas
Trader Joe's Broccoli slaw	Organic raisins
So Delicious coconut milk	Spectrum Naturals organic mayo
Julian Bakery Paleo bread	Julian Bakery Smart Carb II bread

BREAKFAST

Breakfast is often regarded as the most important meal of the day. Don't skip breakfast! A good breakfast is a great way to start off the day and fuel your body for the day's activities. Skipping breakfast can inhibit muscle growth, lower energy levels, and impair overall performance.

Your muscles store carbohydrates in the form of glycogen. The overnight fast depletes some of the muscles' glycogen so this is a great time to have some quality carbohydrates such as, fruits which also provide phytonutrients and antioxidants.

CHOCOLATE YOGURT OATS

Ingredients:
1 cup plain Greek yogurt (I use Fage Total 2%)
½ cup oats
2 Tbsp unsweetened cocoa
2 Tbsp raw cane sugar

Add oats to the yogurt and mix thoroughly. Then, add the cocoa and sugar. For an extra boost, try adding a teaspoon of instant espresso and a little milk.

YOGURT AND COTTAGE CHEESE

Ingredients:
8 ounces plain Greek yogurt
8 ounces lowfat cottage cheese
1 tbsp honey or agave nectar
1 tsp Truvia

Mix the Greek yogurt and cottage cheese together. Add the honey and Truvia to sweeten. You can also add fruit such as, blueberries, strawberries, orange slices, grapes, etc. to add some vitamins and antioxidants. One of my favorites is with raisins and cinnamon.

POWER TOAST

Ingredients:
4 slices whole wheat bread
3 large eggs
1 scoop BioSteel vanilla whey protein
½ teaspoon ground cinnamon
2 Tbsp coconut oil
maple or agave syrup

Heat pan on medium heat with coconut oil.
Whisk the eggs while slowly adding the protein powder.
Dip each slice of bread into the egg mixture for about 30 seconds on each side. Place each slice on a pan and fry until brown on both sides.

MANCAKES

½ cup whole wheat flour
½ all-purpose flour
1 ½ scoop BioSteel whey protein
½ cup quick oats
½ baking soda baking
½ baking powder
½ tsp salt
¾ cup lowfat milk
¼ cup plain yogurt
1 egg
1 Tbsp Earth Balance coconut spread

Mix flour, protein powder, oats, baking soda, baking powder and salt. Slowly add in milk, yogurt, and egg. Mix thoroughly.
Melt coconut spread or on Medium heat. Butter can also substitute coconut spread. Pour a small amount of batter onto the pan. When tiny bubbles appear on the top of the pancake it will be ready to flip. This is usually about 1 to 3 minutes. Cook on the other side for another 1 to 2 minutes. Pancakes should be golden brown on each side. Reapply a small amount of butter or coconut spread to the pan for each pancake.

STUFFED TOAST

4 slices whole grain bread
3 eggs
½ cup lowfat milk
2 Tbsp shredded unsweetened coconut
1 tsp cinnamon
½ tsp vanilla
2 Tbsp coconut oil

Filling:
½ cup plain Greek yogurt
6 strawberries, halved
½ banana
½ tsp vanilla
1 ½ tsp Truvia or 2 tsp cane sugar

Heat pan on medium with coconut oil.
In a mixing bowl, whisk together eggs, milk, coconut, cinnamon and vanilla.
Place each piece of bread in the mixture for at least 30 seconds and place onto the pan. Fry on each side until brown on both sides.

STRAWBERRY CHEESECAKE OATMEAL

Ingredients:
1 cup quick oatmeal
½ cup lowfat milk
½ cup Greek yogurt (Fage Total 2%)
¼ cup reduced fat cream cheese
½ cup strawberries
½ tsp vanilla
1 tsp agave nectar
4 graham crackers, crumbled

Heat the milk in a saucepan on medium heat. Bring to a boil. Add the oatmeal, yogurt, cream cheese, strawberries, vanilla, and agave nectar and cook for additional two minutes. Mix in crumbled graham crackers and serve.

PROTEIN OATMEAL

Ingredients:
1 cup water
¾ cup organic quick oats
1 ½ scoops whey protein powder
½ cup milk
1 tsp Truvia
1 tsp ground cinnamon
1 banana, sliced

Boil 1 cup water on high heat. Mix dry ingredients in a bowl. Add boiling water and milk then mix. Top with sliced banana.

BREAKFAST SMOOTHIE

Ingredients:
1 cup almond milk
½ cup pineapple juice
½ cup pineapple
1 cup kale, chopped
½ cup spinach, chopped
¼ cup parsley sprigs
1 banana

Mix all ingredients in a blender and blend on high for about 30 seconds.

BANANA CREPES

Ingredients:
1 cup all purpose flour
1 banana
2 eggs
½ cup lowfat milk
¼ cup water
2 Tbsp butter, melted
1 Tbsp butter (for the pan)

Whisk the eggs and flour together. Add in the milk and water and continue whisking until smooth. Mix in the butter. Mash 1/2 of the banana and mix in. Heat the remaining butter in a pan on medium heat. Pour the batter into the pan, about 1/4 to 1/2 cup for each crepe. Cook on each side for about two minutes or until golden brown on each side.
Slice other 1/2 of the banana and use for topping. Add a small amount of maple or agave syrup for more sweetness.

BREAKFAST BURRITO

Ingredients:
6 eggs
¼ cup milk
1 lb ground turkey
½ cup refried beans
½ medium onion, chopped
½ tomato, chopped
spinach leaves
½ cup shredded cheddar cheese
spinach tortillas

Beat eggs and milk. Pour into a pan and cook over low-medium heat. Let the eggs set for about a minute then begin gently pulling the eggs from the outside toward the center using a wooden spoon. Distribute the runny parts onto the pan. Continue this process until there are no more runny parts.
Brown ground turkey in a skillet. Wrap all ingredients in spinach tortillas.

BLUE LINE OMELETE

Ingredients:
4-6 large eggs
¼ cup milk
½ onion, finely chopped
½ bell pepper, chopped
½ tomato, chopped
½ cup shredded

Melt 1 Tbsp butter in a pan on medium heat. Add the vegetables and cook for about 5 minutes. Pour the eggs over the vegetables and cook until bottom side is set.
Gently flip the omelet over and cook for another 2 minutes or until that side is set. Add the shredded cheese and fold in half.

COCONUT PANCAKES

4 eggs
3 Tablespoons pasture butter
¼ cup coconut milk
½ cup water
1 Tbsp raw honey
¾ cup coconut flour
1 tsp baking powder

Whisk eggs, coconut milk and honey. Mix the flour and baking powder in a separate bowl. Slowly add the wet ingredients and stir until smooth. Add water in small increments until the desired consistency is achieved. Melt butter on a pan over medium heat then cook pancakes until they are lightly browned on both sides which should take about 3-4 minutes.

LUNCH

Lunch is often a tricky meal especially for hockey players that work or go to school. It's best to cook your own meals if you have time or pack your lunch. This is the time that many hockey players resort to fast food. The extra time you take preparing a lunch the night before will be worth it.
A healthy lunch should consist of slow-digesting, low glycemic index carbohydrates, lean protein and healthy fats to keep blood sugar stable and sustain energy for the middle of the day.

BREADED ZUCCHINI WITH YOGURT SAUCE

Ingredients:
1 medium zucchini
½ cup whole wheat flour
¼ cup olive oil
½ tsp salt

Sauce:
1 cup plain Greek yogurt (Fage Total 0%)
¼ tsp garlic powder
¼ tsp onion powder
¼ tsp salt
¼ tsp black pepper

Cut off the ends of the zucchini and cut into slices. Heat the oil in a pan over medium heat. Dip each slice of zucchini into the flour, covering both sides. Place onto the frying pan. Flip after about 2-3 minutes.

To make the dipping sauce, simply mix together all ingredients in a small bowl.

TUNA ROLLS

Ingredients:
1 can tuna
½ cup whole wheat bread crumbs
¼ cup tartar sauce
½ cup onion, chopped

Preheat oven to 375 degrees. Mix together all ingredients and roll into a ball. Place on a cookie sheet and bake for 15-20 minutes.

POMEGRANATE BERRY PARFAIT

Ingredients:
1 cup Greek yogurt
½ cup pomegranate seeds
½ cup blueberries
½ cup strawberries
½ cup granola
Natural By Nature whipped cream

Mix pomegranate seeds, blueberries, strawberries and granola into yogurt. Top with Natural By Nature whipped cream. If you want to get fancy, serve it in a pretty glass and alternate layers of yogurt and fruit/granola mix.

FRUIT SALAD WITH ORANGE CREAM

Ingredients:
½ cup whipped lowfat cream cheese
½ cup plain Greek yogurt
1 Tbsp honey
2 tsp Truvia
½ tsp natural orange flavoring
1 tsp vanilla
½ cup strawberries
½ banana
½ cup blueberries
¼ cup slivered almonds

Whip together cream cheese yogurt, honey, Truvia, orange flavoring, and vanilla. Mix in the fruits and almonds.

TOP SHELF GAZPACHO

Ingredients:
2 cups chopped tomatoes
1 bell pepper
1 medium red onion, diced
1 cup chopped cucumber
1 ½ cup tomato juice
2 Tbsp lemon juice
2 Tbsp olive oil
1 Tbsp red wine vinegar
2 cloves chopped garlic
1 tsp salt

Combine the tomatoes, pepper, onion and cucumber in a large bowl and mix well. Add the tomato juice, lemon juice, olive oil, vinegar, garlic and salt to the vegetables in a large bowl and mix to combine. Refrigerate for two hours.

BUTTERY FAVA BEANS

Ingredients:
1 can Westbrae Natural fava beans
2 Tbsp Earth Balance buttery spread
1 Tbsp lemon juice
½ tsp garlic powder
½ tsp onion powder
½ tsp oregano
½ tsp rosemary
¼ tsp black pepper
¼ tsp ginger

Melt butter in a medium size pot over medium heat. Add all the spices and stir thoroughly. Cook for about 5 minutes.

ELVIS SANDWICH

Ingredients:
2 whole grain slices bread
2 Tbsp peanut butter
1 banana, sliced

This is a great "weight gainer" for those that have trouble getting enough calories. Carry a couple around in an insulated lunchbox and eat them between meals.

Spread peanut butter evenly on both slices of bread. Cut banana into small slices and place on the peanut butter. Enjoy like this or another option is to toast both sides for a few minutes in a lightly buttered pan.

WALDORF SALAD

Ingredients:
3 apples, chopped
1 Tbsp lemon juice
½ cup walnuts
½ cup raisins
½ cup grapes
3 ribs celery, chopped
½ cup mayonnaise
1 tsp Truvia

In a medium bowl, mix the apples and lemon juice. Add the walnuts, raisins, celery, and grapes.
In a small bowl, mix together the mayonnaise and Truvia. Mix evenly into the other ingredients so everything is covered.

TUNA SALAD

Ingredients:
1 can white tuna
1 hard- boiled egg
2 stalks celery, chopped
¼ cup onions, chopped
3 Tbsp mayonnaise
1 tsp mustard

Hard boil the egg by placing it in a pan and covering it with water. Put the pan on high heat and allow to boil for 10 minutes. Remove the eggs from the pan and place in cold water until ready to crack.

Mix together tuna, chopped celery, chopped onions, mayonnaise, mustard, and eggs. Enjoy this by itself or spread onto two slices of whole grain bread to make a tuna salad sandwich.

PUMPKIN APPLE SOUP

Ingredients:
1 cup canned pumpkin
2 apples, chopped
½ cup onion, chopped
2 cups chicken broth
½ cup apple juice
1 rib celery
½ cup milk
¼ cup half and half
2 Tbsp butter
2 Tbsp brown sugar
¼ tsp salt
¼ tsp pepper

In a pan, sauté the chopped apples and onions in 2 Tbsp butter for about 10 minutes.
Combine all remaining ingredients in a large pot and cook over medium high heat. Add apples and onions and cook for ten minutes.

PBJ TOAST

Ingredients:
2 slices whole wheat bread
2 Tbsp natural peanut butter
1 Tbsp grape jelly
1 Tbsp flax seeds

Toast two slices of bread on the medium toaster setting. Immediately spread peanut butter evenly on both slices. Sprinkle flax or chia seeds on peanut butter. Now spread the jelly over top.

ACAI BERRY SMOOTHIE

Ingredients:
1 cup blueberries
1 cup strawberries
1 banana
1 cup Greek yogurt
1 Tbsp chia seeds
1 Tbsp almond butter
1 cup acai juice
½ cup BioSteel whey powder
Ice cubes

Pour acai juice into a blender then add the blueberries and strawberries. Blend on high for 15 seconds then add the remaining ingredients and blend for another 30 seconds.

CHICKEN STIR FRY

Ingredients:
1 lb boneless, skinless chicken
1 cup broccoli
Trader Joe's broccoli slaw
1 small onion, sliced
4 Tbsp sesame oil
¼ tsp ginger powder
¼ tsp garlic powder
1/8 tsp cayenne
¼ cup ginger juice
soy sauce

Heat two tablespoons oil on medium heat. Cut chicken into small strips and place into pan. Cook until no longer pink and add the broccoli, broccoli slaw, and onion. Now add two more tablespoons sesame oil, ginger juice (optional), and seasonings. Cook for about 10 more minutes.

MUSCLE SANDWICH

Ingredients:
1 Tbsp Earth Balance coconut spread
1 Tbsp Trader Joe's cookie butter
1 Tbsp chia seeds
¼ cup raisins
1 Tbsp cocoa powder
½ scoop BioSteel whey protein
2 slices whole grain bread

Mix together all the ingredients to make the spread. Spread evenly onto the two slices of bread.

PRE-WORKOUT

What you eat close to workout time can have a big impact on your performance and energy. Some carbohydrates and quick-assimilating protein such as, whey isolate are recommended. Most fats should be avoided at this time except for those in the form of medium chain triglycerides such as, coconut milk or oil.

Research shows that moderate amounts of caffeine can improve strength and endurance during an exercise session. Excessive caffeine, however, can impair performance. For most individuals, the amount of caffeine in a double espresso is optimal. Some people are very sensitive to caffeine so it's best to start with small amounts to assess tolerance.

Avoid sugary energy drinks because the excess sugar causes an insulin spike which will eventually result in a crash in energy levels and performance.

Water is by far the best sports drink in the world. Increase water intake as workout time nears and drink water throughout the workout, about 10 ounces every 15 minutes. I use BioSteel High Performance Sports Drink during my workouts because it contains, electrolytes, B vitamins, and branched chain amino acids. For long, hard workouts, I may add 1 or two teaspoons of evaporated cane sugar.

COCONUT WHEY SHAKE

Ingredients:
1 scoop Biosteel whey protein
2 cups So Delicious coconut milk
1 banana
Ice

Mix together in a blender and blend on high for about 30 seconds.

BOILED SWEET POTATO

Ingredients:
Sweet potato
1 Tbsp brown sugar
2 Tbsp Earth Balance coconut spread
¼ tsp cinnamon

Boil water on high heat. Place sweet potato in water. It should be fully immersed. Boil on high for 30 to 45 minutes until soft on the inside. A fork should be able to be easily inserted through to the middle.

OVERTIME ENERGY BAR

Ingredients:
½ Quick cooking rolled oats
1 scoop BioSteel whey powder
½ scoop Casein powder
1 Tbsp coconut oil
1 banana, mashed
¼ cup raisins
1 Tbsp molasses
1 tsp cinnamon
½ tsp vanilla extract

Preheat oven to 350 degrees.
Mix oats and protein powders. Next, mash the banana and mix into dry ingredients. Add the coconut oil. Now mix in the molasses, raisins, cinnamon and vanilla. Shape into bars and place onto a cookie sheet. Bake for 15 minutes.

ENERGY DRINK

Ingredients:
2 scoops BioSteel HP Sports Drink
1 scoop caffeine anhydrous powder (200 mg)
1 tsp beta alanine powder (2 grams)
12 ounces water

Mix all ingredients in a shaker and shake well. Drink immediately. Creatine monohydrate could be added to this as well.

MOCHONUT SHAKE

Ingredients:
1 scoop BioSteel whey protein
2 teaspoons instant espresso
½ cup SoDelicious coconut milk
½ cup filtered water
1 tsp unsweetened cocoa
1 ½ tsp Truvia

Mix all ingredients in a shaker and shake well. Drink immediately. Creatine monohydrate or beta alanine could be added to this as well.

GOALIE GRAHAMS

Ingredients:
3 rectangular graham crackers
Earth Balance coconut spread
Pumpkin or apple butter
Raisins

Break graham crackers into squares using the perforations. Spread on the coconut spread. Spread the pumpkin or apple butter over the coconut spread. Top with raisins.

MAYAN ESPRESSO

Ingredients:
¼ cup cocoa powder
½ tsp cinnamon
1/8 tsp cayenne
1 cup flax milk
2 Tbsp instant espresso
1 tsp Truvia

Whisk together cocoa powder, cinnamon, cayenne pepper, and flax milk in a saucepan on medium heat for three minutes. Add espresso and Truvia then continue cooking until hot but, not boiling. Immediately remove from heat and pour into mugs.

POST-WORKOUT

Proper post-workout nutrition is vital for muscle growth and repair. After a workout, the muscles are starving for nutrients. At this time, the most important nutrients are carbohydrates and protein. This is one time of the day where simple sugars are actually desired as they are transported to the muscles quickly to resynthesize glycogen, the muscular storage form of carbohydrates. It is also best to choose a fast-assimilating protein such as, whey isolate. The best post-workout shake I have found is BioSteel Advanced Recovery Formula. It's got a great combination of carbohydrates and protein without artificial flavors and sweeteners. It's also the best tasting shake I've ever had!

Have your shake within 30 minutes of completing your workout. I typically drink mine about 15 minutes after static stretching to allow time for my nervous system to shift from sympathetic to parasympathetic dominance for better digestion. Make it beforehand and store it in a refrigerator or cooler to keep it fresh.

BANANA SPLIT SHAKE

Ingredients:
2 scoops vanilla BioSteel Advanced Recovery
10 ounces flax milk
1 banana
2 Tbsp strawberry jelly
2 Tbsp chocolate syrup

Add all ingredients in a blender and mix on high. Add as ice desired.

PINA COLADA AND WHEY SHAKE

Ingredients:
1 scoop BioSteel whey powder
1 cup pineapple juice
½ cup coconut milk

Put all ingredients in a blender and mix on high for about 30 seconds. Add ice as desired.

PUMPKIN PIE SMOOTHIE

Ingredients:
1 scoop BioSteel vanilla whey protein powder
½ cup canned pumpkin
1 cup lowfat milk
2 teaspoons Truvia
1 ½ tsp cinnamon
¼ tsp nutmeg
¼ tsp cloves
1 tsp vanilla extract
ice cubes

Put all ingredients in a blender and mix on high for about 30 seconds. Add ice as desired.
For additional calories, add crumbled graham crackers and replace the Truvia with 1 raw cane sugar.

ANTI-INFLAMMATORY SMOOTHIE

Ingredients:
1 scoop BioSteel vanilla whey powder
1 cup flax milk
1 cup papaya
½ cup pineapple
½ cup pineapple juice
2 Tbsp flax seeds
1 inch ginger, peeled and grated
¼ tsp turmeric
½ cup ice

Put all ingredients in a blender and mix on high for about 30 seconds.

CHERRY BERRY SMOOTHIE

Ingredients:
1 scoop BioSteel vanilla whey powder
1 cup tart cherry juice
½ cup almond milk
½ cup blueberries1
½ cup strawberries
½ cup raspberries
2 Tbsp honey
½ cup ice

OATMEAL RAISIN COOKIES

Ingredients:
1 cup whole wheat pastry flour
2 cups rolled oats
3 scoops BioSteel whey powder
1 cup raisins
¾ tsp baking soda
¾ tsp baking powder
½ tsp salt
1 tbsp cinnamon
½ tsp nutmeg
1 cup unsweetened apple sauce
¾ cup egg whites

Preheat the oven to 350F
Mix all dry ingredients in a large bowl. Mix the egg whites and applesauce in a separate bowl. Slowly add the wet ingredients to the dry ingredients. Add in the raisins and continue mixing.
Drop by spoonfuls onto a baking sheet lined with parchment paper
Bake for about 15 minutes. The cookies should be golden brown.

PRE-GAME

This meal can dramatically influence play by maximizing energy levels. It is also best to experiment with different food combinations that suit each particular individual. It's not advised to make a dramatic change prior to a game. This can have disastrous effects. Try them out before a practice to see what works for you.

The pre-game meal should be eaten 2-4 hours before game time. Since carbohydrates are the primary fuel for hockey, they should comprise a large portion of the meal. These carbohydrates should have a low to moderate glycemic load to avoid a spike in insulin which will have a resultant crash. The following recipes have a moderate glycemic load but consult a glycemic load chart for other choices. This meal should also provide some protein and minimal fat.

BAKED CHICKEN AND QUINOA

Ingredients:
2 boneless skinless chicken breasts
1 cup organic quinoa
¼ cup green onions
2 Tbsp olive oil
2 Tbsp honey
¼ cup reduced sodium soy sauce
1/8 tsp cayenne
¼ tsp garlic powder

Preheat the oven to 375 degrees F. Cover a cookie sheet with foil. Place the chicken on the cookie sheet and bake for 30 min. Remove from the oven and flip the breasts. Bake for an additional 30 min.

To cook the quinoa, put 1 cup quinoa and 2 cups water in a saucepan. Bring to a boil then reduce heat to low, added chopped green onions and cover. Cook until all the water is absorbed, about 10-15 minutes. Watch carefully, or it will burn shortly after the water has been absorbed.

In another saucepan, mix the oil, honey, soy sauce, cayenne and garlic powder. Cook on medium until hot but, not boiling. Pour over chicken and quinoa.

WHOLE WHEAT SPAGHETTI AND MEATBALLS

Ingredients:
3 ounces whole wheat pasta
1 cup pasta sauce
1lb ground beef
1 egg
¼ cup whole wheat bread crumbs
¼ cup chopped onion
¼ tsp salt
¼ tsp pepper

Preheat oven to 350 F. In a bowl, combine the egg, bread crumbs, onion, salt, and pepper. Add the beef and mush with hands to mix ingredients thoroughly. Form into balls and place on a baking sheet. Bake for about 30 minutes or until meat is no longer pink.

Prepare the pasta according to the package directions which is, typically boiling for about 10-12 minutes. I would recommend serving the pasta al dente which is slightly firm. This retains more of the nutrients.

GAME 7 STEAK AND POTATO

Ingredients:
1 lb boneless top sirloin steak
1 cup mushrooms
¼ salt
2 Tbsp butter
¼ pepper
1 russet potato
2 Tbsp olive oil
butter or sour cream

Preheat oven to 425 degrees F. Scrub potato and rub with olive oil. Wrap the potato in aluminum foil and bake for about 50 minutes or until you can easily slide a fork through. Top with grass fed butter or light sour cream.
Sauté onions in 2 Tbsp butter and set aside.
Place steak in a pan and cook on medium heat for two minutes. Flip over and flip for two more minutes. Add the mushrooms and continue cooking for two minutes on each side until the inside of the steak is no longer pink.

TUNA CASSEROLE

Ingredients:
1 cup whole wheat rotini
½ cup plain Greek yogurt
½ cup reduced fat sour cream
1 ½ cups cheddar cheese
2 cups frozen peas
1 can tuna
½ cup whole wheat bread crumbs
½ tsp sea salt
½ tsp pepper

Preheat oven to 450 degrees.
Cook pasta in a saucepan according to package instructions. Add the frozen peas with about two minutes left. Drain and set aside.
Mix together yogurt, sour cream, cheese, salt and pepper. Add the cooked pasta and peas when ready. Pour into a baking dish coated with cooking spray. Cover with bread crumbs and cook for about 8-10 minutes.

SHEPHERD'S PIE

Ingredients:
1 lb lean grass-fed beef
2 large sweet potatoes
1/2 cup peas
½ cup onion, chopped
½ cup tomato sauce
2 Tbsp Worcestershire sauce
2 Tbsp lowfat milk
2 Tbsp butter
½ tsp cinnamon
½ tsp salt
½ tsp black pepper
1/8 tsp cayenne

Boil a large pan of water. Add sweet potatoes and boil for about 30-45 minutes until a fork slides easily through the baked potatoes. Mash the sweet potatoes. Add in the butter and the milk and mix. Now mix in the peas, onion, tomato sauce cinnamon, and Worcestershire sauce,
Preheat oven to 400 degrees.
Cook ground beef over medium heat until brown. Put in a glass baking dish. Cover the beef with the potato mixture. Bake for 30 minutes.

DINNER

A balanced dinner helps nourish the body and provides ample nutrients to help the body recover from the day's activities and provides energy for the remainder of the day. Many hockey players make the mistake of eating a little here and there throughout the day and try to get in all their calories at dinner. This puts excess stress on the digestive system and doesn't allow for proper absorption of nutrients. Choose a lean protein (chicken), a vegetable for a side and a slow-digesting carbohydrate (sweet potato).

LEMON CHICKEN AND BROWN RICE

Ingredients:
1 lb boneless skinless chicken breast
2 Tbsp extra virgin olive oil
¼ cup lemon juice
2 Tbsp honey
1 tsp rosemary
¼ tsp black pepper
¼ tsp salt
lemon slices (optional)
¼ cup brown rice
1 Tbsp grass fed butter

Preheat oven to 400 degrees F. Place chicken breasts in a baking dish. Pour lemon juice over the chicken allowing the remaining juice to settle at the bottom of the dish. Brush chicken with olive oil then pour the honey onto the chicken. Sprinkle the salt and pepper and put lemon slices on top of the chicken. Bake in the oven for 30 minutes.
Prepare the rice according to the package and flavor with grass fed butter.

SAUSAGE MEATLOAF

Ingredients:
1 lb ground spicy chorizo sausage
½ lb grass fed ground beef
1 egg
1 onion, chopped
1 cup whole wheat bread crumbs
1 cup lowfat milk
1 Tbsp brown sugar
2 Tbsp mustard
½ tsp salt
½ tsp pepper

Preheat oven to 350 degrees F. Mix the beef, egg, onion, milk, salt, pepper, and bread crumbs in a large bowl. Place in a 5x9 inch loaf pan or a baking dish. Mix the brown sugar, ketchup, and mustard. Pour this mixture over the meat loaf.
Bake the loaf for one hour at 350 degrees F.

FOURTH LINE BURGER AND SWEET POTATO FRIES

Ingredients:
1 lb lean grass fed beef
1 egg
¼ cup whole wheat bread crumbs
(I use Whole Foods 365 brand)
¼ onion, finely chopped

2 large sweet potatoes
2 tsp salt
2 tsp pepper
¼ tsp cayenne pepper
2 tsp garlic powder
3 Tbsp extra virgin olive oil

Whisk egg with seasonings. Mix in beef and bread crumbs. Separate into 4 patties and cook on medium heat for about 20 minutes or until brown all the way through.
Top with mustard, ketchup and hot sauce. No buns.

Fries:
Preheat oven to 450 degrees. Cut sweet potato into thin slices. Mix all spices in a shallow dish. Coat the sweet potato slices in the olive oil and roll in the spices until covered. Place on a cooking sheet and bake for 15 minutes. Flip the fries over and cook for another 10-15 minutes.

MEATHEAD STUFFED PEPPERS

Ingredients:
4 bell peppers
½ tsp olive oil
1 pound lean ground beef
1 egg white
½ cup finely chopped yellow onion
¼ cup toasted wheat germ
½ tsp black pepper
½ tsp cayenne pepper
½ cup tomato sauce

Preheat oven to 425 degrees. Cut off the tops of the peppers and remove all seeds. Coat the skins lightly with the olive oil. Place the peppers on a baking pan with the open side down and bake for about 10 minutes. Reduce heat to 350 degrees.
Mix the beef, onion, wheat germ, black pepper, cayenne pepper, 21 Seasoning Salute , and tomato sauce.

PARMESAN TURKEY

Ingredients:
1 lb turkey cutlets
1 egg
½ cup whole wheat bread crumbs
½ cup parmesan cheese
½ tsp sea salt
½ tsp pepper
1 Tbsp extra virgin olive oil

In a bowl, beat the egg. In another bowl, mix bread crumbs, parmesan cheese, salt and pepper.
Heat the oil on medium heat in a frying pan.
Dip each cutlet into the beaten egg then dip into the dry mixture. Place cutlets into pan and cook until there is no pink on the inside, about 10-12 minutes. Turn over every 2-3 minutes.
Serve with vegetables.

FISH AND CHIPS

Ingredients:
1 ½ Tsp extra virgin olive oil
2 cod fillets
1 tsp Trader Joe's 21 Seasoning Salute
½ lemon
2 sweet potatoes
½ tsp oregano
½ tsp salt
¼ tsp pepper

To make the chips: preheat the oven to 450 degrees. Cut the sweet potatoes into thin slices. Place on a cooking sheet and pour oil 2 Tbsp oil over the slices. Sprinkle on oregano, salt, and pepper. Bake for 30-40 minutes depending on desired crispiness.
To make the fish: pour 1/2 Tbsp oil into a shallow baking dish allow to spread around the entire dish. Sprinkle the seasoning onto the fillets. Squeeze the juice of the lemon over the filets. Bake for 8 to 10 minutes.

BAKED PINEAPPLE CHICKEN

Ingredients:
2 lbs chicken breasts
¼ cup yellow onions, sliced
¼ cup green onions, chopped
½ cup pineapple juice
½ cup crushed pineapple
¼ cup candied ginger
1 tsp rosemary
½ tsp salt
¼ tsp pepper

Preheat oven to 375 degrees. Place the chicken in a baking dish. Cover with sliced onions. Combine pineapple juice, crushed pineapple, candied ginger, rosemary, salt, and pepper. Pour this mixture over the chicken and cook for about 45 minutes.

SLOPPY BROS

Ingredients:
1 lb grass fed ground beef
2 Tbsp Worcestershire sauce
½ cup carrots, minced
1 medium onion, chopped
3 ribs celery, diced
1 cup tomato sauce
¼ cup green pepper
¼ cup ketchup
½ tsp mustard powder
½ tsp garlic powder
2 tsp brown sugar
whole wheat buns

In a pan, cook beef over medium heat until brown. Stir in Worcestershire sauce, carrots, onion, celery, tomatoes sauce, green pepper, ketchup, mustard powder, garlic powder, and brown sugar. Bring to a boil then reduce heat to low and simmer while covered for 15-20 minutes.

GUINNESS BEEF

Ingredients:
1 Tbsp olive oil
2 lb chuck roast
½ tsp sea salt
¼ tsp black pepper
2 Tbsp red wine vinegar
4 yellow onions, sliced
1 can Guinness
1 Tbsp Worcestershire sauce

Heat the oil in a large skillet over high heat. Season the chuck all over with salt and pepper. Add the beef to the pan and sear until all sides are browned, about 10 minutes. Remove the beef; add the vinegar, onions, and beer to the pan.
Place the beef in the base of a slow cooker and pour the onions and beer over then the Worcestershire sauce. Cook on low for 6 hours.

HEALTHY SNACKS

Snacks are often important for staving off hunger. They can also provide energy and maintain stable blood sugar levels between your regular meals. Ingesting your total calories for the day in the form of three large meals can leave you hungry for hours and your energy may wane during that time. Snacks also provide your muscles with a continuous flow of nutrients to help them repair and adapt to training. A handful of nuts or raw fruits and vegetables can make great snacks. Homemade trail mix with fruits and nuts is also a great option because it gives you a combination of quick and slow energy sources. Prepare snacks ahead of time and carry them with you.

BRANDON'S TASTY TREATS

Ingredients:
½ scoop BioSteel whey
1 Tbsp Earth Balance buttery spread
2 Tbsp Earth Balance coconut spread
2 Tbsp almond butter
¼ cup raisins
1 Tbsp unsweetened shredded coconut
2 Tbsp semi-sweet chocolate chips
2 Tbsp chia seeds

Mix together almond butter and coconut spread. Slowly add protein powder while mixing. Mix in the raisins and coconut. Refrigerate for about 30 minutes. These are a good choice any time of day but are a particularly great late night snack.

GREEN BEANS WITH ALMONDS

Ingredients:
1 pound green beans, fresh or frozen, not canned
1 teaspoon extra virgin olive oil
sea salt
¾ cup slivered almonds

Bring a large pot of water to a boil. Add green beans and boil for 2-3 minutes. Drain.
Add the oil and salt and toss.
Coat the almonds lightly with butter. Heat over medium heat for about 3 minutes. Add the beans and cook for about 3 minutes.

ALMOND BUTTER APPLES

Ingredients:
1 apple, any variety
2 Tbsp

Cut apple into slices. Spread on the almond butter and enjoy this simple, healthy snack.

DEVILED EGGS

Ingredients:
6 eggs
2 Tbsp mayonnaise
1 tsp mustard
1 tsp white vinegar
¼ tsp salt

First, hard boil eggs by placing them in a saucepan and covering with cold water. Bring to a boil on high heat. Remove from the heat and cover the pan. Allow eggs to sit for 12 minutes then immerse in cold water. Cut all eggs in half and remove yolks. Set the whites aside. Mash the yolks with a fork and add mustard, vinegar, and salt. Now put this mixture into the egg white halves.

OLIVE-FILLED TOMATOES

Ingredients:
10 cherry tomatoes
10 pitted olives
10 small slices mozzarella cheese

Cut the top off each tomato and scoop out the center of the tomato. Place an olive and a small slice of mozzarella cheese in the open center of each tomato.

STUFFED CELERY

Ingredients:
3 stalks celery
3 Tbsp peanut butter
¼ cup raisins

Wash and cut celery stalks in half. Spread the peanut butter evenly through the stalks. Top with raisins. Another great option is to use whipped cream cheese with a little agave nectar in place of the peanut butter.

APPLE SAUCE

Ingredients:
4 apples, cored and peeled
2 tsp lemon juice
¼ cup honey
¾ cup water
½ tsp cinnamon
Pinch salt

In a saucepan, combine water and apples and cook covered over medium heat for about 20 minutes until apples are soft. When the apples are soft, remove from heat and mash the apples with a fork or potato masher. Add the lemon juice, honey, cinnamon and salt then allow to cool.

HEALTHY SCRATCH

Ingredients:
¼ cup cashews
¼ cup almonds
¼ cup peanuts
¼ cup dark chocolate chips
¼ cup dried cranberries
1/8 cup unsweetened coconut flakes

This is a great snack to have with you for bus trips. Just combine all ingredients and mix together. Store in a BPA container.

BAKED APPLES

Ingredients:
2 apples
2 Tbsp walnuts
2 Tbsp raisins
2 tsp cinnamon

Preheat oven to 375 degrees F. Core and peel the apples from the bottom. Mix together walnuts, raisins and cinnamon. Stuff the mixture into the apples. Sprinkle additional cinnamon over the apples. Place into a glass baking dish with about an inch of water on the bottom. Bake for 30 minutes.

ROASTED NUTS

Ingredients:
¼ cup almonds
¼ cup pecans
¼ cup walnuts
1 Tbsp grass fed butter
¼ cup honey
½ tsp cinnamon

In a saucepan, combine honey, butter and cinnamon. Bring to a boil. Pour over nuts and place them on a cookie sheet. Bake for 10 minutes at 350 degrees F. Sprinkle additional cinnamon over the nuts.

JACKED WEIGHT GAIN SHAKE

Ingredients:
3 Scoops BioSteel Advanced Recovery
16 ounces lowfat milk
1 banana
1 scoop vanilla ice cream
2 Tbsp almond butter
1 teaspoon creatine powder

First blend the milk and BioSteel. Then add in the banana, almond butter and ice cream.

VICTORY PARTY RECOVERY DRINK
Ingredients:
2 scoops BioSteel HP sports drink
½ cup orange juice
20 ounces Smart Water
1 Tablespoon flax oil

This is a very quick and easy drink. Just mix everything together and enjoy.

LATE NIGHT ANTICATABOLIC SHAKE

This is especially important for those that have trouble building muscle or can't stay asleep because of hunger.

Ingredients:
¾ scoop casein protein powder
¼ scoop BioSteel whey powder
1 Tbsp coconut flour
1 Tbsp oat flour
½ cup lowfat milk
½ cup water
ice (optional)

This one is a bit too thick to mix in a regular shaker so you should use a blender. Combine all ingredients in the blender and mix on high for 30 seconds.

CHEAT MEALS

It's alright to occasionally indulge in a cheat meal. This can provide a much needed psychological break from a strict diet and allow you to enjoy some of your favorite foods. One meal will have little effect on your training. Good nutrition can take some discipline but it's not necessary to deprive yourself. I try to schedule a cheat meal about once a week. It's important not to do this much more often than this. Don't start having a daily cheat meal or an entire cheat day. Don't overstuff yourself either. Most importantly, don't have your cheat meal before a game or workout. This can be disastrous. Enjoy your cheat meal but, be reasonable.

CHIPOTLE FRYBURGERS

Ingredients:
1 lb grass fed beef
1 egg
¼ cup bread crumbs
French fries
2 Tbsp mayonnaise
chipotle hot sauce
ketchup
buns

Whisk egg with seasonings. Mix in beef and bread crumbs. Separate into 4 patties and cook on medium heat for about 20 minutes or until brown all the way through.
Mix together mayonnaise and chipotle hot sauce.
Prepare French fries according to package directions. Coordinate the cooking time so the fries and burgers are done at the same time.
Place burgers on buns. Put ketchup on burgers. Top with fries then chipotle mayo sauce.

BISON CHILI CHEESE FRIES

Ingredients:
½ package frozen organic French fries
8 ounces shredded cheddar cheese
1 pound ground bison
1 large onion, finely chopped
1 large carrot, finely chopped
3 stalks of celery, chopped
1 medium green bell pepper, finely chopped
3 large garlic cloves, finely chopped
½ tsp cinnamon
2 tsp ground cumin
2 tsp chili powder
1 Tbsp apple cider vinegar
1 can diced tomatoes
1 can crushed tomatoes
1 can kidney beans, drained and rinsed

Prepare the French fries according to the directions on the package.
Brown meat in a skillet then add onion, carrot, celery, pepper and garlic and sauté for 5-7 minutes. Put bison and sautéed vegetable mixture to a large pot and add beans, tomatoes, apple cider vinegar and spices. Simmer for 40 minutes, stirring occasionally.

Pour the hot chili over the fries. Sprinkle the cheese over the chili.

PBJ SUPER PANCAKES

Ingredients:
2 slices bread
2 Tbsp peanut butter
2 Tbsp grape jelly
½ cup all-purpose flour
1 Tbsp raw cane sugar
1 Tbsp baking powder
½ tsp salt
1 egg, beaten
½ cup milk
½ Tbsp vegetable oil

Spread peanut butter and jelly onto bread. Mix all other ingredients together using a wire whisk. Melt butter on pan over medium heat. Dip peanut butter and jelly sandwich into batter for 30 seconds on each side and place into pan. Pour the remaining batter over the sandwich. Flip when the batter begins to bubble.

CREATINE COOKIES

Ingredients:
2 ½ cups all-purpose flour
¼ cup coconut flour
1 teaspoon baking soda
½ tsp baking powder
1 cup Earth Balance coconut spread, softened
1 ½ cups white sugar
1 egg
1 tsp vanilla extract
Icing:
½ cup powdered sugar
1 Tbsp milk
1 tsp vanilla
¼ cup unsweetened shredded coconut
1 tsp creatine powder

Preheat oven to 375 degrees. In a bowl, mix butter and sugar then beat in the egg. Slowly add the dry ingredients. Roll into balls and place on a cookie sheet. Bake for 8 to 10 minutes.
Preparing icing:
Mix together all ingredients until smooth. For more thickness, add a small amount of corn starch until desired thickness is reached.

EATING ON THE ROAD

Before I travel anywhere, I plan ahead by searching online for nearby healthy grocery stores such as, Whole Foods and Trader Joes. I'll stock up my hotel room with all my meals for each day of the trip. I always try to get a room with a fridge and a kitchenette.

Smoothie chains such as, Smoothie King and Jamba Juice have become popular stops for travelling hockey players. Although, smoothies are made mostly of fruits and vegetables, they are often high in sugar. This may make them better options for after games.

Eating out may not be the best option but when travelling with a team, sometimes it's the only option. Following is a list of popular restaurants and some of the healthier options on their menu.

- Don't be afraid to ask for what you want. Make special requests if you need to.
- Drink water or unsweetened iced tea instead of soda or sugary drinks.
- Choose meals that are steamed, baked, broiled or grilled instead of those that are fried or sautéed.

- Stay away from descriptions such as, breaded, crispy or creamy.
- Choose a low fat protein such as, chicken breast or fish as the main dish.
- Choose a high-quality carbohydrate such as, brown rice or sweet potato as a side as well as, two different vegetables.
- Fruit such as, grapes or orange slices can be a great dessert.
- Ask for whole wheat bread for sandwiches.
- Ask for salad dressing and sauces on the side and only use half or less.
- Don't feel like you have to clear your plate. Most restaurants give excessive portions of cheap foods like pasta.
- Look up the menu online and figure out the healthiest options ahead of time.

Chipotle- Fajita bowl, black beans, half serving brown rice, any meat, mild and medium salsa, light sour cream, and light on the cheese.

Noodles and Company- Bangkok curry with shrimp

Bob Evans- Grilled salmon fillet, steamed broccoli, baby carrots, and applesauce

IHOP- Simple and Fit spinach, mushroom, and tomato omelet with one or two whole wheat pancakes

Panera's/St. Louis Bread Co- Smoked Turkey breast sandwich on wheat bread and summer fruit cup

Boston Market- Half chicken with garlicky lemon spinach, green beans, and steamed vegetables

Applebee's- Grilled jalapeno lime shrimp

Arby's- Pecan chicken salad on whole grain wrap

Cracker Barrel- Grilled sirloin steak, baked potato, and vegetables

QDoba- three crispy tacos, pork, mild and medium salsa, guacamole, and cheese

Subway- Chipotle steak and cheese with avocado on honey oat bread, light on the chipotle sauce

Smoothie King- 32 ounce Skinny Activator, any flavor, Hulk for weight gain or post-workout

Jamba Juice- Berry UpBeet smoothie with whey protein boost

Starbucks- Protein Box

ALDAN PERFORMANCE

Aldan Performance is a strength and conditioning business dedicated to enhancing the performance of hockey players of all levels and abilities from youth to pro. Aldan Performance utilizes advanced training models based on the latest research in sports science. Currently, there are off-ice training programs available for those living in the St. Louis area as well as, web-based training programs for any hockey player anywhere in the world.

Check out www.aldanperformance.com for more information about programs that can take your game to the next level.

Made in the USA
Lexington, KY
06 September 2014